THE TIME TO LOSE JOURNAL

This journal belongs to

Date started

Date completed

This journal is dedicated to my husband Fred and our two sons, who love me unconditionally, my diet counselor and friend, Deborah Burns-Davidian, as well as Sarah Gewanter, Denny Cooper, Michelle Ognibene, Joelle Clark, and to everyone who is coping with a weight challenge.

Other Journals by Jan Yager, Ph.D.
*Friendship Journal: A Journal With Selected Quotes about Friendship from
    Friendshifts,® and a Journal*
Personal Journal: Blank Book With Ruled Pages
Everything Notebook: Business Journal/ Blank Book With Ruled Pages
Birthday Book: A Journal

Selected Books by Jan Yager, Ph.D.
Friendshifts®: The Power of Friendship and How It Shapes our Lives
Creative Time Management for the New Millennium
Creative Time Management
Business Protocol
Making Your Office Work for You
How to Write Like a Professional
The Help Book
Victims
Single in America
Meatless Cooking: Celebrity Style
Untimely Death: A Novel (co-authored with Fred Yager)
The Cantaloupe Cat: A Picture Book (illustrated by Mitzi Lyman)

The Time to Lose Journal

Cover art, introduction, poetry, text, and interior design by Jan Yager, Ph.D.
Copyright 2000 by Jan Yager, Ph.D.
ISBN 1-889262-66-8 (hardcover)
ISBN 1-889262-67-6 (trade paperback)
Published by:
Hannacroix Creek Books, Inc.
1127 High Ridge Road, PMB 110
Stamford, CT 06905-1203
(203) 321-8674 FAX (203) 968-0193
E-mail: Hannacroix@aol.com
On the web: www.Hannacroix.com

Printed in the United States of America

THE TIME TO LOSE JOURNAL

Developed by
Jan Yager, Ph.D.
Author of
Creative Weight Management: An Audio Book
Creative Time Management for the New Millennium

Hannacroix Creek Books, Inc.   Stamford, CT

WARNING - DISCLAIMER

Foreword by Jan Yager, Ph.D.

I developed this journal because I want to help others who are also battling a weight problem. Losing 77 pounds in 10 months over the last year--from 213 to my goal of 136--and keeping it off, has been a challenge and an achievement.

Keeping a journal helped me to stay motivated and on track. Writing down why I was eating, as well as what I was eating, in addition to planning meals and menus, helped me to have a clear idea of what to buy when I shopped for the foods that would keep me focused on my weight loss program.

My personal success using a journal to lose, and keep off, weight is mirrored by the results of 38 dieters monitored by psychologists Raymond C. Baker, Ph.D. and Daniel S. Kirschenbaum, Ph.D. As reported in the July 1998 issue of the American Psychological Association's *Health Psychology*, those dieters who wrote in a journal, recording all the food they ate as well as the calories in those foods, had better control over their weight during the holidays (Thanksgiving, Christmas/Hanukah, and New Year's Eve) than those who did not keep a journal.

This journal is, first and foremost, your personal weight management workbook. It is intended as just one of the many tools to help you face, and overcome, your weight management and exercise challenges. In addition to writing in this journal you will certainly want to get a medical checkup before beginning your weight loss program. You will also want to follow a medically-sound weight loss program that includes regular professional monitoring of your progress.

Everyone asks me what I did to lose the weight. Of course I followed a medically-sound supervised weight loss program. My weight loss counselors helped educate me about what to eat and their support helped me to stay motivated.

But I had done that before, only to regain the weight. Why was I losing the weight far more readily this time, with a lot less resistance and angst? Why was I able to get back on track on my weight program after a "bad day" instead of giving up completely?

What was I doing differently this time that I am maintaining my 77 pound weight loss rather than going right back up the scale?

The answer is that this time I trained myself to apply the principles of my time management research and knowledge to my weight loss and maintenance efforts. In *Creative Weight Management: An Audio Book* and in my forthcoming book, *Time to Lose: Using Creative Time Management Skills to Finally Win Your Battle With Weight*, the 7 principles of creative weight management are discussed in detail. I am not a nutritionist, but I am a sociologist, researcher, and time management consultant. What I can share with you are the 7 principles of creative *weight* management that I developed, and follow, by using creative *time* management principles to cope with the weight management challenge:

7 Principles of Creative Weight Management

1. *Focus. Decide to take action and do something about your weight.*
2. *Prioritize this weight challenge as your #1 concern.*
3. *Get a medical check up.*
4. *Pick a medically-sound, supervised plan that you will follow; plan, shop, and prepare for each meal, each day.*
5. *Create more manageable goals, rewarding yourself as you go down the scale, as you lose the next smaller unit of weight out of the total you have to lose, such as each 1, 3, 5, or 10 pound loss.*
6. *Include exercise, and non-food stress reducers, such as keeping a journal, into each day.*
7. *When you reach your goal weight, make maintaining your weight loss your new #1 priority and goal.*

This journal will help you put into practice these 7 principles of creative weight management by making a daily commitment to your weight challenge. For most of us, losing weight, and keeping it off, requires a concerted effort. The weight rarely comes off "on its own." Losing weight, and keeping it off, is more likely to be achieved by making this weight challenge your number #1 priority.

It is also important to note that since everyone's weight issues are unique #3, "get a medical check-up" is a key principle to Creative Weight Management as well as #4, "Pick a medically-sound, supervised weight loss program that you will follow." Following those principles will help your long-term weight loss, and maintenance, success. The basic weight loss advice of eating less and exercising has to be applied by a weight expert (doctor, nurse, nutritionist, trained weight loss professional) to just *you* -- your body composition, activity level, and any medical or emotional issues that your weight management program needs to address.

Another key benefit of keeping a journal: it makes it easier to document just what you are putting into your mouth. As anyone with a weight challenge will attest, it is usually all-too-easy to "snack" or eat far more than you thought you were eating unless you carefully document the portions, and foods, that you are eating.

After 3 days of pre-weight program logs, to help you assess just how much you are currently eating, and when, there is a page where, if you wish, you could place a "before" picture as well as your starting, and goal, weights. There's a "Checklist for Day One," as well as an original poem, "Just for Today," that might help you to get through a particularly difficult day during your diet.

In addition to a "Weekly Menu" page for planning the meals for the week, there are daily logs for two months providing a place to track exactly what you are eating for all three meals, plus snacks, water intake, vitamins, as well as exercising. There are also enough additional blank ruled pages for writing or framed unruled pages for drawing for a 3rd month or even a lot longer.

Keeping this journal is just one of many tools to help you lose weight and keep it off. Trying to lose weight and keep it off is a positive action: research has linked being overweight to an increased likelihood of cancer, heart disease, and diabetes.

Maintaining this weight loss diary may be beneficial just because it takes some of the energy you might have put into overeating and focuses it on another action, writing and reflecting.

You may want your *Time to Lose Journal* to be completely personal and private or you may want to share it with others, such as your diet counselor or physician. Don't worry about the spelling or grammar in your entries. This journal is for *you* as a tool for your weight challenge.

Here's what you'll find in this journal:
--making time to exercise
--"Before" Food Logs for 3 days
--a checklist for day one
--"Just for Today" a motivational poem
--A "Before" Picture page
--"Weekly Weigh ins" for 52 weeks
--A place to put your basic weight loss program guidelines
--Weekly Menu planner (you will find a blank one before each week of daily entry pages
--Two months of one-page-per-day daily food and exercise logs (breakfast, lunch, dinner, snacks, vitamins, water) with room at the bottom of each page for recording thoughts, observations, etc. as well as additional blank ruled and unruled pages to record notes or food diaries for at least another month or even a lot longer.
-- A place for several favorite lower-calorie recipes
-- An "After" Picture page.
-- A place to record your Maintenance Plan.

So start writing (or drawing), and starting losing!

For additional motivation, check out *Creative Weight Management: An Audio Book* by Jan Yager, Ph.D. (60 minutes) (Hannacroix Creek Books, Inc., 1999; $14.95 retail list price, available at local or on-line bookstores or directly from Book Clearing House by calling, toll-free, 800-431-1579). For further personal and work time management suggestions, see *Creative Time Management for the New Millennium* by Jan Yager, Ph.D. (Hannacroix Creek Books, Inc., 1999; $28.95 hardcover, $14.95 trade paperback, available at local or on-line bookstores or directly from the publisher through Book Clearing House by calling, toll-free, 800-431-1579).

MAKING TIME TO EXERCISE

In order to make finding time to exercise a priority for you, take a few moments to write down why it's important for you to exercise.

Reasons why it is important for me to exercise:

1. _____ .
2. _____ .
3. _____ .

Once you accept that it is paramount to your overall self-improvement and weight management plan to exercise, your next step is to make the time even if it means parking your car farther away so you force yourself to start walking (be careful about your personal safety, however, and make sure you won't have to walk long distances in deserted areas or alone late at night), dancing in your home or apartment, taking an exercise class, or increasing your participation in family or group sports or athletic activities.

On the journal pages that follow for two months of day-to-day recordings, you will find a place for keeping track of your daily exercise activities.

"BEFORE" FOOD LOGS

A key time management tool to help someone gain better control of his or her time is to ask a client to fill out time logs so someone could document and visibly see just where his or her time is "going."

Similarly, these Food Logs could help you to keep track of what you are currently eating *before* you begin your weight loss program.

What are you eating NOW? Do you know when, or why, you overeat? Are you aware of how often you snack?

Make copies of these logs if you want to track more than 3 days. Or if you're already beginning a weight loss program, skip these logs and go right to the next section which provides two complete months of daily logs to use while you are following a weight loss program.

WHAT ARE YOU CURRENTLY EATING? USE THESE FOOD LOGS TO FIND OUT

Today is _____ Today's date _____

Just like time logs that provide information on how time is being spent, use these food logs to find out when you are eating, and what, as preparation for beginning a creative weight management program or just to learn more about your eating habits. If possible, note when you are eating, and even where (kitchen table? dining room? standing up at the kitchen counter? at your desk at work?) You might also note what you are feeling when you are eating, e.g. Hungry? Starved? Bored? Lonely? Sad? Happy? Angry? Stressed? Frustrated?

LOG #1

Breakfast   WHEN   WHAT   WHERE   WHY

_____

_____

_____

Lunch   WHEN   WHAT   WHERE   WHY

_____

_____

_____

Dinner   WHEN   WHAT   WHERE   WHY

_____

_____

_____

Snacks   WHEN   WHAT   WHERE   WHY

_____

_____

_____

Water _____

Vitamins _____

Exercise _____

_____

_____

_____

WHAT ARE YOU CURRENTLY EATING? USE THESE FOOD LOGS TO FIND OUT

Today is _____ Today's date _____

Breakfast   WHEN   WHAT   WHERE   WHY | LOG #2 |

_____

_____

_____

Lunch   WHEN   WHAT   WHERE   WHY

_____

_____

Dinner   WHEN   WHAT   WHERE   WHY

_____

_____

_____

Snacks   WHEN   WHAT   WHERE   WHY

_____

_____

Water

_____

Vitamins

_____

Exercise

_____

_____

_____

Breakfast   WHEN   WHAT   WHERE   WHY   LOG #3

_____

_____

_____

Lunch   WHEN   WHAT   WHERE   WHY

_____

_____

_____

Dinner   WHEN   WHAT   WHERE   WHY

_____

_____

_____

_____

Snacks   WHEN   WHAT   WHERE   WHY

_____

_____

_____

Water

_____

Vitamins

_____

Exercise

_____

_____

_____

CheckList for Day One

To help your creative weight management program's success, and to make sure you find *Time to Lose*, you need to do whatever works for you that's medically sound and supervised by a qualified weight-loss professional. Do you function better if you get rid of all the foods in your house or apartment that cause you to lose control, or is it better to have it around so you can say 'no' to it? Do you have all the foods you need on hand, or do you need to go to the supermarket or fresh fruit and vegetable stand?

Here are some considerations:

1. Have I gone through my refrigerator and pantry getting rid of anything that I think will sabotage my weight management program?

2. Have I gone shopping for everything I think I should have on hand that will be helpful to me?

3. Have I decided when I will weigh in?

4. Do I want to take a "Before" picture? If I do , have I done that yet?

5. How will I handle this weight management plan? Will I tell others about it, or keep it to myself? Will I try to find a partner to diet along with me, or do it on my own?

6. What do I need to do to make this Day One successful for me? measuring spoons? measuring cups? a food scale to be able to more accurately track portions?

_____

_____

This poem may help you to stay focused on your weight challenge, a day at a time.

Just For Today
by Jan Yager

Just for today I'll try my best
Just for today.

Just for today
I'll focus on now and not the rest
Just for today.

Just for today
I'll count my blessings.
Just for today
I'll count my fingers and my toes.

Just for today
I'll think of someone less fortunate.
Just for today
I'll hug those I love.

Just for today
I'll look at the bright side.
Just for today
I'll think of all that I've achieved.

Just for today
I'll try not to complain.

Just for today.
Just for today.

BEFORE PICTURE

Starting date

_____

Starting weight

_____

Goal weight

_____

WEEKLY WEIGH INS

Starting weight _____   Difference (+ or -)

Week 1	_____	
Week 2	_____	_____
Week 3	_____	_____
Week 4	_____	_____
Week 5	_____	_____
Week 6	_____	_____
Week 7	_____	_____
Week 8	_____	_____
Week 9	_____	_____
Week 10	_____	_____
Week 11	_____	_____
Week 12	_____	_____
Week 13	_____	_____
Week 14	_____	_____
Week 15	_____	_____
Week 16	_____	_____
Week 17	_____	_____
Week 18	_____	_____
Week 19	_____	_____
Week 20	_____	_____
Week 21	_____	_____
Week 22	_____	_____
Week 23	_____	_____
Week 24	_____	_____
Week 25	_____	_____
Week 26	_____	_____
Week 27	_____	_____
Week 28	_____	_____
Week 29	_____	_____

Weekly weigh ins (continued)Difference (+ or -)

Week 30 _____ _____
Week 31 _____ _____
Week 32 _____ _____
Week 33 _____ _____
Week 34 _____ _____
Week 35 _____ _____
Week 36 _____ _____
Week 37 _____ _____
Week 38 _____ _____
Week 39 _____ _____
Week 40 _____ _____
Week 41 _____ _____
Week 42 _____ _____
Week 43 _____ _____
Week 44 _____ _____
Week 45 _____ _____
Week 46 _____ _____
Week 47 _____ _____
Week 48 _____ _____
Week 49 _____ _____
Week 50 _____ _____
Week 51 _____ _____
Week 52 _____ _____

YOUR WEIGHT MANAGEMENT
PROGRAM GUIDELINES

USE THIS PAGE TO WRITE DOWN THE DETAILS
OF THE WEIGHT LOSS PROGRAM YOU ARE
FOLLOWING (OR ATTACH A COPY OF YOUR
PROGRAM GUIDELINES)

_____

_____

_____

_____

_____

_____

_____

_____

_____

_____

_____

_____

_____

_____

_____

_____

_____

_____

_____

_____

_____

_____

_____

WEEKLY MENU

Monday

Tuesday

Wednesday

Thursday

Friday

Saturday

Sunday

Daily Time to Lose/Creative Weight Management Journal Entries

Today is _____   Today's date _____

Any special challenges today? Yes___ No ____
If yes, those challenges are: _____

Breakfast

Lunch

Dinner

Water

Snacks

Vitamins

Exercise

Notes/Comments

Daily Time to Lose/Creative Weight Management Journal Entries

Today is _____   Today's date _____

Any special challenges today? Yes___ No ____
If yes, those challenges are: _____

Breakfast

Lunch

Dinner

Water

Snacks

Vitamins

Exercise

Notes/Comments

Daily Time to Lose/Creative Weight Management Journal Entries

Today is _____   Today's date _____

Any special challenges today? Yes___ No ____
If yes, those challenges are: _____

Breakfast

Lunch

Dinner

Water

Snacks

Vitamins

Exercise

Notes/Comments

Daily Time to Lose/Creative Weight Management Journal Entries

Today is _____ Today's date _____

Any special challenges today? Yes___ No ____
If yes, those challenges are: _____

Breakfast

Lunch

Dinner

Water

Snacks

Vitamins

Exercise

Notes/Comments

Daily Time to Lose/Creative Weight Managemen
Journal Entries

Today is _____ Today's date _____

Any special challenges today? Yes___ No ____
If yes, those challenges are: _____

__Breakfast__

__Lunch__

__Dinner__

Water

Snacks

Vitamins

Exercise

Notes/Comments

Daily Time to Lose/Creative Weight Management
Journal Entries

Today is _____   Today's date _____

Any special challenges today? Yes___ No ___
If yes, those challenges are: _____

Breakfast

Lunch

Dinner

Water

Snacks

Vitamins

Exercise

Notes/Comments

Daily Time to Lose/Creative Weight Management Journal Entries

Today is _____   Today's date _____

Any special challenges today? Yes___ No ____
If yes, those challenges are: _____

_____ Breakfast _____

_____ Lunch _____

_____ Dinner _____

_____ Water _____

_____ Snacks _____

_____ Vitamins _____

_____ Exercise _____

_____ Notes/Comments _____

WEEKLY MENU

Monday

Tuesday

Wednesday

Thursday

Friday

Saturday

Sunday

Daily Time to Lose/Creative Weight Managemen
Journal Entries

Today is _____   Today's date _____

Any special challenges today? Yes___ No ____
If yes, those challenges are: _____

Breakfast

Lunch

Dinner

Water

Snacks

Vitamins

Exercise

Notes/Comments

Daily Time to Lose/Creative Weight Management Journal Entries

Today is _____   Today's date _____

Any special challenges today? Yes___ No ____
If yes, those challenges are: _____

_____

Breakfast

_____

Lunch

_____

_____

Dinner

_____

_____

_____

_____

Water

Snacks

Vitamins

Exercise

_____

Notes/Comments

_____

_____

_____

_____

_____

_____

_____

_____

Daily Time to Lose/Creative Weight Management Journal Entries

Today is _____   Today's date _____

Any special challenges today? Yes___ No ____
If yes, those challenges are: _____

Breakfast

Lunch

Dinner

Water

Snacks

Vitamins

Exercise

Notes/Comments

Daily Time to Lose/Creative Weight Management
Journal Entries

Today is _____   Today's date _____

Any special challenges today? Yes___ No ____
If yes, those challenges are: _____

Breakfast _____

Lunch _____

Dinner _____

Water _____

Snacks _____

Vitamins _____

Exercise _____

Notes/Comments _____

Daily Time to Lose/Creative Weight Management Journal Entries

Today is _____ Today's date _____

Any special challenges today? Yes___ No ____
If yes, those challenges are: _____

Breakfast

Lunch

Dinner

Water

Snacks

Vitamins

Exercise

Notes/Comments

Daily Time to Lose/Creative Weight Management Journal Entries

Today is _____ Today's date _____

Any special challenges today? Yes___ No ____
If yes, those challenges are: _____

Breakfast

Lunch

Dinner

Water

Snacks

Vitamins

Exercise

Notes/Comments

Daily Time to Lose/Creative Weight Management Journal Entries

Today is _____ Today's date _____

Any special challenges today? Yes___ No ____
If yes, those challenges are: _____

Breakfast

Lunch

Dinner

Water

Snacks

Vitamins

Exercise

Notes/Comments

WEEKLY MENU

Monday

Tuesday

Wednesday

Thursday

Friday

Saturday

Sunday

Daily Time to Lose/Creative Weight Management Journal Entries

Today is _____   Today's date _____

Any special challenges today? Yes___ No ____
If yes, those challenges are: _____

Breakfast

Lunch

Dinner

Water

Snacks

Vitamins

Exercise

Notes/Comments

Daily Time to Lose/Creative Weight Management
Journal Entries

Today is _____   Today's date _____

Any special challenges today? Yes___ No ____
If yes, those challenges are: _____

_____

Breakfast _____

_____

Lunch _____

_____

_____

Dinner _____

_____

_____

_____

_____

Water _____

Snacks _____

Vitamins _____

Exercise _____

_____

Notes/Comments _____

_____

_____

_____

_____

_____

_____

_____

Daily Time to Lose/Creative Weight Management
Journal Entries

Today is _____   Today's date _____

Any special challenges today? Yes___ No ___
If yes, those challenges are: _____

Breakfast

Lunch

Dinner

Water

Snacks

Vitamins

Exercise

Notes/Comments

Daily Time to Lose/Creative Weight Management
Journal Entries

Today is _____   Today's date _____

Any special challenges today? Yes___ No ____
If yes, those challenges are: _____

Breakfast

   Lunch

   Dinner

   Water

   Snacks

   Vitamins

   Exercise

   Notes/Comments

Daily Time to Lose/Creative Weight Management Journal Entries

Today is _____   Today's date _____

Any special challenges today? Yes___ No ____
If yes, those challenges are: _____

Breakfast

Lunch

Dinner

Water

Snacks

Vitamins

Exercise

Notes/Comments

Daily Time to Lose/Creative Weight Management
Journal Entries

Today is _____   Today's date _____

Any special challenges today? Yes___ No ___
If yes, those challenges are: _____

_____

_____ Breakfast _____

_____

_____ Lunch _____

_____

_____

_____

_____ Dinner _____

_____

_____

_____

_____

_____

_____ Water _____

_____ Snacks _____

_____ Vitamins _____

_____ Exercise _____

_____

_____ Notes/Comments _____

_____

_____

_____

_____

_____

_____

_____

_____

_____

Daily Time to Lose/Creative Weight Management Journal Entries

Today is _____   Today's date _____

Any special challenges today? Yes___ No ____
If yes, those challenges are: _____

_____

Breakfast _____

_____

Lunch _____

_____

_____

Dinner _____

_____

_____

_____

_____ .

_____

Water _____

Snacks _____

Vitamins _____

Exercise _____

_____

Notes/Comments _____

_____

_____

_____

_____

_____

_____

_____

_____

_____

WEEKLY MENU

Monday

Tuesday

Wednesday

Thursday

Friday

Saturday

Sunday

Daily Time to Lose/Creative Weight Managemen
Journal Entries

Today is _____   Today's date _____

Any special challenges today? Yes___ No ____
If yes, those challenges are: _____

Breakfast

Lunch

Dinner

Water

Snacks

Vitamins

Exercise

Notes/Comments

Daily Time to Lose/Creative Weight Management Journal Entries

Today is _____   Today's date _____

Any special challenges today? Yes___ No ____
If yes, those challenges are: _____

Breakfast
_____

Lunch
_____
_____

Dinner
_____
_____
_____
_____

Water
Snacks
Vitamins
Exercise
_____

Notes/Comments
_____
_____
_____
_____
_____
_____
_____

Daily Time to Lose/Creative Weight Management Journal Entries

Today is _____   Today's date _____

Any special challenges today? Yes___ No ___
If yes, those challenges are: _____

Breakfast

Lunch

Dinner

Water

Snacks

Vitamins

Exercise

Notes/Comments

Daily Time to Lose/Creative Weight Management Journal Entries

Today is _____   Today's date _____

Any special challenges today? Yes___ No ____
If yes, those challenges are: _____

_____

Breakfast _____

_____

  Lunch _____

_____

_____

  Dinner _____

_____

_____

_____

_____

  Water _____

  Snacks _____

  Vitamins _____

  Exercise _____

_____

  Notes/Comments _____

_____

_____

_____

_____

_____

_____

_____

_____

_____

Daily Time to Lose/Creative Weight Managemen Journal Entries

Today is _____   Today's date _____

Any special challenges today? Yes___ No ____
If yes, those challenges are: _____

Breakfast

Lunch

Dinner

Water

Snacks

Vitamins

Exercise

Notes/Comments

Daily Time to Lose/Creative Weight Management Journal Entries

Today is _____   Today's date _____

Any special challenges today? Yes___ No ____
If yes, those challenges are: _____

Breakfast

Lunch

Dinner

Water

Snacks

Vitamins

Exercise

Notes/Comments

Daily Time to Lose/Creative Weight Management
Journal Entries

Today is _____   Today's date _____

Any special challenges today? Yes___ No ___
If yes, those challenges are: _____

Breakfast

Lunch

Dinner

Water

Snacks

Vitamins

Exercise

Notes/Comments

WEEKLY MENU

Monday

Tuesday

Wednesday

Thursday

Friday

Saturday

Sunday

Daily Time to Lose/Creative Weight Management
Journal Entries

Today is _____ Today's date _____

Any special challenges today? Yes___ No ____
If yes, those challenges are: _____

Breakfast

Lunch

Dinner

Water

Snacks

Vitamins

Exercise

Notes/Comments

Daily Time to Lose/Creative Weight Management
Journal Entries

Today is _____   Today's date _____

Any special challenges today? Yes___ No ____
If yes, those challenges are: _____

Breakfast

Lunch

Dinner

Water

Snacks

Vitamins

Exercise

Notes/Comments

Daily Time to Lose/Creative Weight Management Journal Entries

Today is _____ Today's date _____

Any special challenges today? Yes___ No ___
If yes, those challenges are: _____

Breakfast

Lunch

Dinner

Water

Snacks

Vitamins

Exercise

Notes/Comments

Daily Time to Lose/Creative Weight Management Journal Entries

Today is _____   Today's date _____

Any special challenges today? Yes___ No ___
If yes, those challenges are: _____

Breakfast

Lunch

Dinner

Water

Snacks

Vitamins

Exercise

Notes/Comments

Daily Time to Lose/Creative Weight Management Journal Entries

Today is _____   Today's date _____

Any special challenges today? Yes___ No ___
If yes, those challenges are: _____

Breakfast

Lunch

Dinner

Water

Snacks

Vitamins

Exercise

Notes/Comments

Daily Time to Lose/Creative Weight Management
Journal Entries

Today is _____   Today's date _____

Any special challenges today? Yes___ No ____
If yes, those challenges are: _____

Breakfast _____

    Lunch _____

    Dinner _____

    Water _____

    Snacks _____

    Vitamins _____

    Exercise _____

    Notes/Comments _____

Daily Time to Lose/Creative Weight Management Journal Entries

Today is _____   Today's date _____

Any special challenges today? Yes___ No ____
If yes, those challenges are: _____

_____

Breakfast _____

_____

Lunch _____

_____

_____

Dinner _____

_____

_____

_____

_____

Water _____

Snacks _____

Vitamins _____

Exercise _____

_____

Notes/Comments

_____

_____

_____

_____

_____

_____

_____

_____

WEEKLY MENU

Monday

Tuesday

Wednesday

Thursday

Friday

Saturday

Sunday

Daily Time to Lose/Creative Weight Managemen Journal Entries

Today is _____   Today's date _____

Any special challenges today? Yes___ No ____
If yes, those challenges are: _____

Breakfast

Lunch

Dinner

Water

Snacks

Vitamins

Exercise

Notes/Comments

Daily Time to Lose/Creative Weight Management Journal Entries

Today is _____   Today's date _____

Any special challenges today? Yes___ No ____
If yes, those challenges are: _____

Breakfast

Lunch

Dinner

Water

Snacks

Vitamins

Exercise

Notes/Comments

Daily Time to Lose/Creative Weight Management Journal Entries

Today is _____   Today's date _____

Any special challenges today? Yes___ No ____
If yes, those challenges are: _____

Breakfast

Lunch

Dinner

Water

Snacks

Vitamins

Exercise

Notes/Comments

Daily Time to Lose/Creative Weight Management Journal Entries

Today is _____   Today's date _____

Any special challenges today? Yes___ No ____
If yes, those challenges are: _____

Breakfast

Lunch

Dinner

Water

Snacks

Vitamins

Exercise

Notes/Comments

Daily Time to Lose/Creative Weight Management Journal Entries

Today is _____   Today's date _____

Any special challenges today? Yes___ No ___
If yes, those challenges are: _____

Breakfast

Lunch

Dinner

Water

Snacks

Vitamins

Exercise

Notes/Comments

Daily Time to Lose/Creative Weight Management Journal Entries

Today is _____   Today's date _____

Any special challenges today? Yes___ No ____
If yes, those challenges are: _____

_____
_____ **Breakfast** _____
_____
_____
_____ **Lunch** _____
_____
_____
_____
_____ **Dinner** _____
_____
_____
_____
_____
_____
_____ **Water** _____
_____ **Snacks** _____
_____ **Vitamins** _____
_____ **Exercise** _____
_____
_____ **Notes/Comments** _____
_____
_____
_____
_____
_____
_____
_____
_____

Daily Time to Lose/Creative Weight Management Journal Entries

Today is _____   Today's date _____

Any special challenges today? Yes___ No ____
If yes, those challenges are: _____

Breakfast

Lunch

Dinner

Water

Snacks

Vitamins

Exercise

Notes/Comments

WEEKLY MENU

Monday

Tuesday

Wednesday

Thursday

Friday

Saturday

Sunday

Daily Time to Lose/Creative Weight Management Journal Entries

Today is _____   Today's date _____

Any special challenges today? Yes___ No ___
If yes, those challenges are: _____

_____ **Breakfast** _____

_____ **Lunch** _____

_____ **Dinner** _____

_____ **Water**
_____ **Snacks**
_____ **Vitamins**
_____ **Exercise**

_____ **Notes/Comments**

Daily Time to Lose/Creative Weight Management Journal Entries

Today is _____   Today's date _____

Any special challenges today? Yes___ No ___
If yes, those challenges are: _____

Breakfast

Lunch

Dinner

Water

Snacks

Vitamins

Exercise

Notes/Comments

Daily Time to Lose/Creative Weight Management Journal Entries

Today is _____   Today's date _____

Any special challenges today? Yes___ No ____
If yes, those challenges are: _____

Breakfast

Lunch

Dinner

Water

Snacks

Vitamins

Exercise

Notes/Comments

Daily Time to Lose/Creative Weight Management
Journal Entries

Today is _____   Today's date _____

Any special challenges today? Yes___ No ____
If yes, those challenges are: _____

Breakfast

Lunch

Dinner

Water

Snacks

Vitamins

Exercise

Notes/Comments

Daily Time to Lose/Creative Weight Management Journal Entries

Today is _____   Today's date _____

Any special challenges today? Yes___ No ____
If yes, those challenges are: _____

Breakfast

Lunch

Dinner

Water

Snacks

Vitamins

Exercise

Notes/Comments

Daily Time to Lose/Creative Weight Management Journal Entries

Today is _____   Today's date _____

Any special challenges today? Yes____ No ____
If yes, those challenges are: _____

Breakfast

Lunch

Dinner

Water

Snacks

Vitamins

Exercise

Notes/Comments

Daily Time to Lose/Creative Weight Management
Journal Entries

Today is _____   Today's date _____

Any special challenges today? Yes___ No ___
If yes, those challenges are: _____

Breakfast

Lunch

Dinner

Water

Snacks

Vitamins

Exercise

Notes/Comments

WEEKLY MENU

Monday

Tuesday

Wednesday

Thursday

Friday

Saturday

Sunday

Daily Time to Lose/Creative Weight Management Journal Entries

Today is _____   Today's date _____

Any special challenges today? Yes___ No ____
If yes, those challenges are: _____

Breakfast

Lunch

Dinner

Water

Snacks

Vitamins

Exercise

Notes/Comments

Daily Time to Lose/Creative Weight Management Journal Entries

Today is _____   Today's date _____

Any special challenges today? Yes___ No ___
If yes, those challenges are: _____

_____

__**Breakfast**_____

_____

__**Lunch**_____

_____

_____

__**Dinner**_____

_____

_____

_____

_____

__**Water**_____

__**Snacks**_____

__**Vitamins**_____

__**Exercise**_____

_____

__**Notes/Comments**_____

_____

_____

_____

_____

_____

_____

_____

_____

_____

Daily Time to Lose/Creative Weight Management Journal Entries

Today is _____   Today's date _____

Any special challenges today? Yes___ No ___
If yes, those challenges are: _____

Breakfast

Lunch

Dinner

Water

Snacks

Vitamins

Exercise

Notes/Comments

Daily Time to Lose/Creative Weight Management
Journal Entries

Today is _____   Today's date _____

Any special challenges today? Yes___ No ____
If yes, those challenges are: _____

Breakfast

Lunch

Dinner

Water

Snacks

Vitamins

Exercise

Notes/Comments

Daily Time to Lose/Creative Weight Management Journal Entries

Today is _____   Today's date _____

Any special challenges today? Yes___ No ____
If yes, those challenges are: _____

Breakfast

Lunch

Dinner

Water

Snacks

Vitamins

Exercise

Notes/Comments

Daily Time to Lose/Creative Weight Management Journal Entries

Today is _____   Today's date _____

Any special challenges today? Yes___ No ____
If yes, those challenges are: _____

Breakfast

Lunch

Dinner

Water

Snacks

Vitamins

Exercise

Notes/Comments

Daily Time to Lose/Creative Weight Management Journal Entries

Today is _____   Today's date _____

Any special challenges today? Yes___ No ___
If yes, those challenges are: _____

Breakfast

Lunch

Dinner

Water

Snacks

Vitamins

Exercise

Notes/Comments

WEEKLY MENU

Monday

Tuesday

Wednesday

Thursday

Friday

Saturday

Sunday

Daily Time to Lose/Creative Weight Management
Journal Entries

Today is _____   Today's date _____

Any special challenges today? Yes___ No ____
If yes, those challenges are: _____

Breakfast

Lunch

Dinner

Water

Snacks

Vitamins

Exercise

Notes/Comments

Daily Time to Lose/Creative Weight Management Journal Entries

Today is _____   Today's date _____

Any special challenges today? Yes____ No ____
If yes, those challenges are: _____

_____

Breakfast

_____

   Lunch

_____

_____

   Dinner

_____

_____

_____

_____

   Water

   Snacks

   Vitamins

   Exercise

_____

   Notes/Comments

_____

_____

_____

_____

_____

_____

_____

Daily Time to Lose/Creative Weight Management Journal Entries

Today is _____ Today's date _____

Any special challenges today? Yes___ No ____
If yes, those challenges are: _____

Breakfast

Lunch

Dinner

Water

Snacks

Vitamins

Exercise

Notes/Comments

Daily Time to Lose/Creative Weight Management
Journal Entries

Today is _____ Today's date _____

Any special challenges today? Yes___ No ____
If yes, those challenges are: _____

Breakfast

Lunch

Dinner

Water

Snacks

Vitamins

Exercise

Notes/Comments

Daily Time to Lose/Creative Weight Management
Journal Entries

Today is _____   Today's date _____

Any special challenges today? Yes___ No ___
If yes, those challenges are: _____

Breakfast

Lunch

Dinner

Water

Snacks

Vitamins

Exercise

Notes/Comments

Daily Time to Lose/Creative Weight Management Journal Entries

Today is _____   Today's date _____

Any special challenges today? Yes___ No ____
If yes, those challenges are: _____

Breakfast _____

Lunch _____

Dinner _____

Water _____
Snacks _____
Vitamins _____
Exercise _____

Notes/Comments _____

Daily Time to Lose/Creative Weight Management Journal Entries

Today is _____   Today's date _____

Any special challenges today? Yes___ No ___
If yes, those challenges are: _____

Breakfast

Lunch

Dinner

Water

Snacks

Vitamins

Exercise

Notes/Comments

WEEKLY MENU

Monday

___

Tuesday

___

Wednesday

___

Thursday

___

Friday

___

Saturday

___

Sunday

NOTES

NOTES

NOTES

NOTES

NOTES

NOTES

NOTES

NOTES

NOTES

NOTES

NOTES

NOTES

NOTES

NOTES

NOTES

NOTES

NOTES

NOTES

NOTES

NOTES

NOTES

NOTES

NOTES

FAVORITE
LOWER CALORIE
RECIPES

Recipe for

Recipe for

Recipe for
_____

AFTER PICTURE

Date

Weight

```
******************************************************
*                                                    *
*              MAINTENANCE  PLAN                      *
*                                                    *
*   (A crucial element to an effective weight loss program to help avoid   *
*   the yo-yo syndrome — of losing and then regaining the lost weight)   *
*                                                    *
*                                                    *
******************************************************
```

_____

_____

_____

_____

_____

_____

_____

_____

_____

_____

_____

_____

_____

_____

_____

_____

_____

_____

_____

_____

_____

_____

_____

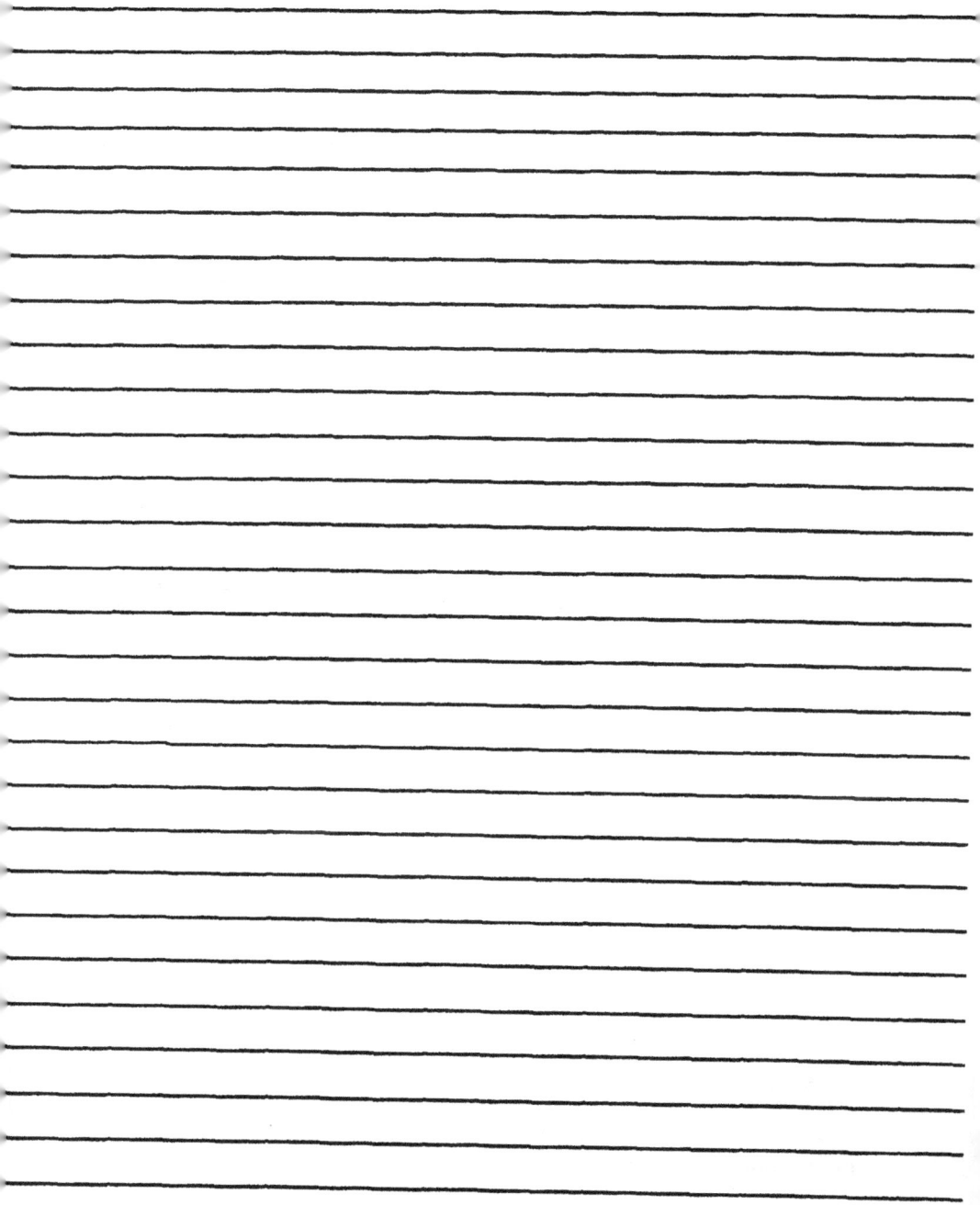

Also available from Hannacroix Creek Books--
CREATIVE WEIGHT MANAGEMENT: An Audio Book
Winning the Weight Battle by Applying Creative Time Management Principles to Your Weight Management Challenge
By Jan Yager, Ph.D.

In this motivational tape, *Creative Weight Management*, time management consultant, author, and sociologist Jan Yager discusses the innovative weight management program she developed based on an application of her time management principles to the weight management challenge.

By applying the principles espoused in this tape, as she followed a supervised diet program with weekly weigh-ins, and kept a diet journal, Dr. Yager was readily able to lose 77 pounds—from 213 to 136 — in 10 months (from a size 18 to a size 6).

Here's what they're saying about this audio book:
> "We wholeheartedly endorse *Creative Weight Management: An Audio Book*. This tape explains the innovative way that time management expert Dr. Jan Yager applies the key principles of effective and creative time management to the weight challenge. Her inspirational story provides hope and help to those who want to lose weight and keep it off.
> "
> --Sarah Gewanter, LCSW, Clinical Director, Darien Diet Center

> "Bravo to Dr. Jan Yager for providing her useful, innovative time management ideas about how to start, and stick with, a weight loss program in the easily-accessible format of an audio book. I recommend this tape as an excellent reinforcement to the new eating and exercise habits that we teach."
> --Deborah Burns-Davidian, consultant, Darien Diet Center

> "As a former lecturer for a famous weight loss organization, it took me nine years to learn the hard truth as presented by Dr. Yager in this audio book. It is a straight-forward, honest look at the challenges of not only weight loss but weight management...Her seven principles will help anyone attain their goal and structure their future maintenance. This is a must for anyone wanting to lose weight and keep it off!"—Suzanne Vaughan, Professional Speaker and Trainer

Time: 60 minutes
Price: $14.95 ISBN 1-889262-62-5
Available at local or on-line bookstores or directly from the publisher by calling Book Clearing House (800-431-1579).

www.ingramcontent.com/pod-product-compliance
Lightning Source LLC
Chambersburg PA
CBHW031859090426